The Call of the Savior: A Journey Within

Come, weary soul, with burdens deep,

The peace you seek is yours to keep.

There's One who calls with arms
widespread,

A Savior's love, the path ahead.

No need to fear, no need to run,

His light will shine, outshine the sun.

Through every storm, through every fight,

His grace will guide, His love will light.

The world may tempt with fleeting joy,

But Christ alone your soul can buoy.

In Him, your heart will find its rest,

A perfect peace, a love confessed.

His arms are open, full of grace,

He longs to meet you face to face.

So let Him in, and feel the start,

Of hope reborn within your heart.

Don't wait for signs, don't hesitate,

The Savior calls—now is the fate.

Let go of fear, of doubt, of pain,

And in His love, you'll live again.

Accept His call, His mercy free,

And in His heart, you'll truly be.

For Jesus waits with open door,

Come in, be healed, and rest once more.

The Woman at the Well

Beneath the sun at Sychar's well,
A woman came with tales to tell.
Her jar was heavy, her heart the same,
A life of longing, burdened with shame.

A stranger sat with gentle grace,
Lines of wisdom etched on His face.
"Give Me a drink," He softly spoke,
And in her soul, a stirring woke.

"You are a Jew, and I, unclean,
Why speak to me, unseen, demeaned?"
Yet He replied with a truth profound,
"Living water can here be found.

If you but knew the gift I bring,
You'd drink, and never thirst again."
Her questions rose, her wonder grew,
"Are You a prophet? Can this be true?"

He named her past, her hidden strife,
The tangled web of her wounded life.
Yet judgment lay not in His eyes;
Instead, compassion, vast as the skies.

She left her jar, her shame, her pain,
And ran to share what she'd gained:
"Come, see the man who knew it all,
The promised Savior, who heard my call!"

A simple meeting, a life restored,
Her testimony, a harvest soared.
The woman at the well, unknown, unseen,
Became a herald of the King.

Wisdom's Song: The Book of Proverbs

In Proverbs' halls of timeless light,
Wisdom calls through day and night.
Her voice is clear, her counsel pure,
A guiding path, steadfast and sure.

She stands in streets, where fools may stray,
And beckons hearts to learn her way.
"Fear the Lord, the start of all—
The humble rise, the prideful fall."

A gentle word turns wrath aside,
While reckless tongues bring storms to tide.
The sluggard sleeps, the diligent reap,
For toil brings bread, while laziness weeps.

The tongue of truth, a treasure rare,
A fountain of life for those who care.
Yet lies are snares, deceit is vain,
A fleeting joy, a lasting pain.

Like gold refined, the heart must be,
Guard it well, for all flows free.
A cheerful soul brings health and balm,
But envy robs the spirit's calm.

Through thirty-one, her verses ring,
A crown of wisdom for life's king.
For every step, a lamp, a guide,
In faith and love, with God beside.

O Proverbs, book of wisdom's art,
You pierce the mind and stir the heart.
Your timeless truths forever stand,
A gift of grace from God's own hand.

God, the Fortress Breaker

O my God, with hands of grace,

You tear down strongholds, leaving no trace.

Walls built by fear, by doubt, by pain,

Come crumbling down in Your holy name.

Each thought that drifts, each darkened snare,

You seize and hold with tender care.

Captive now to truth's sweet light,

You turn my mind from wrong to right.

The chains of despair once bound my soul,

But Your love whispers, making me whole.

With every promise, you renew my song,

Restoring hope where it's been gone so long.

Spirit weary, crushed by weight,

You breathe new life, you recreate.

Your mercy flows, a healing stream,

Reviving dreams and broken schemes.

O God of hope, my heart You fill,

Your strength restores my wavering will.

No fortress stands, no fear can stay,

When You arise and make a way.

So here I stand, renewed, restored,

With thoughts aligned to Christ my Lord.

My spirit soars, my hope takes flight,

For in Your love, all things turn right.

God's Diamond

I'm not a diamond, flawless, bright,
Unmarked by flaw, reflecting light.
No gleaming gem in perfect form,
No faultless beauty to transform.

Yet in my cracks, my jagged edge,
My broken vows, my faltered pledge,
The Maker sees a treasure rare,
A diamond formed through love and care.

For polished stones by human hand
Are cold, and still, though they may stand.
But God, the Jeweler, sees in me
A work of grace, a masterpiece.

Each flaw, a story, each scar, a song,
Of mercy given when I was wrong.
Each fracture shines with heaven's glow,
A love unearned, yet made to show.

I'm not a diamond for my pride,
Or perfect life I cannot hide.
But in my flaws, His glory gleams,
A radiant hope beyond my dreams.

So take this heart, so rough, untrue,
And shape it, Lord, to shine for You.
For in Your hands, I'm more refined,
A flawed, but cherished, diamond mined.

Golden Threads

In the quiet, where shadows fall,
Among the ruins, tattered and small,
The Master's hands, both gentle and wise,
Weave golden threads through shattered
skies.

A vessel cracked, its beauty lost,
Scattered shards at a bitter cost,
But He kneels low, to gather each piece,
Binding with gold, till sorrows cease.

Through brokenness, a story gleams,
A glimmer of hope in fractured dreams.
The jagged lines, now etched with grace,
Tell of a love time can't erase.

What once was marred, now shines anew,
A masterpiece the Maker drew.
Each thread of gold, each stitch of light,
Transforms the wounds into His might.

For broken things aren't cast away;
They bear the marks of night and day.
In every scar, His beauty glows,
Through every tear, His mercy flows.

So let the world see what was done—
A mosaic of grace beneath the sun.
God's golden weave, both tender and true,
Turns broken things to something new.

In Him Alone

The world will tell us, "You are enough,"
With fleeting truths and empty fluff.
It paints a portrait, grand yet frail,
A treasure built to rot and fail.

We chase the gold, the praise of men,
Yet find ourselves alone again.
Our worth, it wavers, comes and goes,
Like drifting tides or melting snows.

But in the stillness, hear His voice:
"I am your hope, your lasting choice.
Not wealth, nor fame, nor what you do,
Can match the love I've given you."

For on the cross, our worth was sealed,
A sacred truth, by blood revealed.
No earthly claim, no mortal pride,
Could hold the weight of Him who died.

In Jesus' eyes, we find our place,
Not by our merit, but His grace.
A love unearned, a gift so free,
Defines our worth eternally.

So lay your burdens at His feet,
Let striving end, let grace complete.
For all we are, and hope to be,
Is found in Him, our Victory.

Ruth's Song

In fields of Moab, her story began,
A tale of love, of a faithful plan.
A daughter, a widow, a stranger so true,
Her heart bore burdens, yet her hope grew.

When Naomi wept, "Call me no more,
For bitterness reigns where joy was before,"
Ruth clung tightly, her words a vow,
"Your God, my God, I follow now."

Through barley fields in Bethlehem's light,
She gleaned with courage from dawn to night.
A humble labor, her faith her guide,
With Boaz's kindness, grace multiplied.

"Who is this woman, so steadfast, so kind?"
In her gentle spirit, favor did he find.
A redeemer rose, by providence planned,
To shelter Ruth with his outstretched hand.

A lineage born from her sacred choice,
Echoes of mercy in a faithful voice.
Through her line, a King would rise,
To redeem the earth and pierce the skies.

Ruth, the foreigner, yet richly entwined,
In the tapestry of God's design.
A beacon of loyalty, love, and trust,
In her legacy, the faithful adjust.

The Artist's Sky

The sunset spills its golden hues,
A masterpiece in reds and blues.
Brushstrokes blaze as daylight fades,
Painting wonders as shadows invade.

The clouds, like whispers, softly glide,
A canvas stretched both far and wide.
Each stroke of light, a love-designed,
A glimpse of God, the Great Divine.

Then night unveils its velvet veil,
With stars like gems in bright detail.
The heavens speak, though silent still,
Of hands that shape and hearts that will.

But morning breaks with fresh delight,
A tapestry of dawning light.
The pinks and oranges, bold and new,
Declare His mercies ever true.

Each sunrise tells of hope restored,
A whispered song from heaven's Lord.
Each sunset sighs in quiet praise,
A gift of grace for fleeting days.

The skies proclaim what hearts may miss,
That all of this was made for bliss.
God's artwork speaks, both near and far,
Of who we are—and whose we are.

The Beatitudes

On the mount, He spoke with grace,
Words of hope for every place.
Blessed are they, the meek, the low,
Whose hearts reflect His mercy's glow.

Blessed are the poor in spirit's way,
For heaven's kingdom is their stay.
The mourners weep, their hearts oppressed,
But they shall find in God their rest.

Blessed are the meek, the earth their prize,
A gentle heart the world defies.
Those who hunger, thirst for right,
Shall be fulfilled with heaven's light.

Blessed are the merciful and kind,
For mercy's gift in them they'll find.
The pure in heart, their eyes will see
The face of God eternally.

Blessed are the peacemakers, who restore,
For they are children of the Lord.
The persecuted, bruised, reviled,
Their place in heaven is reconciled.

Rejoice, be glad, when trials come near,
For prophets too endured this fear.
In every word, His truth resounds,
A promise sure, where love abounds.

Oh, blessed are the lives so true,
That live His words in all they do.
For in these truths, the Savior's voice,
Gives every heart a cause to rejoice.

The Creator Steps In

Eternal Word, the spark of life,
Breathed galaxies, with voice so rife.
The stars were hung, the oceans stirred,
By whispered will, the living Word.

Yet veiled in time, the Master's plan,
To walk the earth as humble man.
Infinity, in flesh confined,
The Architect of space and mind.

He left the throne, celestial gleam,
To tread the dust of His own dream.
The hands that shaped the mountain's peak,
Now calloused grew, soft words to speak.

The heavens bowed; the angels gazed,
As earth's Redeemer, unamazed,
Was born in straw, beneath the sky,
The Builder chose to live, to die.

Creator's feet on soil tread,
Among the lost, where hope seemed dead.
He healed, He wept, He bore our scars,
The King of Kings beneath the stars.

What love could span such vast divide,
To join creation, stand beside?
The Potter stooped, His work to mend,
The broken clay, His love to end.

And now we see, through manger's glow,
The Maker's heart, come down to show,
That He who spun the worlds above,
Is boundless still, in endless love.

They call Him Shepherd, tending the stray,
Guiding the lost to a brighter way.
With staff in hand and heart so pure,
Through valleys deep, His love endures.

They call Him Savior, breaking chains,
Bearing the weight of sin's dark stains.
On Calvary's hill, His mercy poured,
The perfect Lamb, our risen Lord.

They call Him Healer, binding the soul,
Touching the wounds to make us whole.
With every tear, His hands embrace,
Restoring hope, revealing grace.

They call Him King, the Prince of Peace,
Whose reign of love will never cease.
Upon His brow, the crown may lie,
Yet meek and humble, He draws nigh.

They call Him Light, a guiding flame,
Dispelling shadows in His name.
The Morning Star, so brightly gleams,
Fulfilling every prophet's dreams.

They call Him Friend, so close, so near,
A constant presence, calm and clear.
Through joy and sorrow, night and day,
He walks beside us, come what may.

They call Him Alpha, the first and true,
Beginning of all that's good and new.
Omega too, the final Word,
The timeless God whose voice is heard.

They call Him Jesus, Emmanuel,
God with us here, where we dwell.
No name too great, no name too small,
In every tongue, He's Lord of all.

O holy names, each one a song,
Proclaim His glory loud and strong.
For in each name, the truth is shown:
Jesus, the Christ, our cornerstone.

The Path to Healing

A wound may cut both deep and wide,
A scar that time won't let subside.
The heart, it aches, the spirit cries,
Beneath the weight of bitter ties.

We try to mend with our own hands,
To understand, to make demands.
Yet every effort, every plea,
Falls short of setting captives free.

But in the silence, soft and still,
A voice speaks hope, a higher will:
"Forgive, as I have forgiven you,
Let love redeem what hate once slew."

It isn't ours to bear alone,
For God, in mercy, calls His own.
Through His great strength, our hearts can mend,
And broken souls begin to bend.

Forgiveness flows like healing streams,
Restoring life, reviving dreams.
Not by our power, not by might,
But by His grace, His guiding light.

O Lord, we falter, weak and small,
Yet You are faithful through it all.
Teach us to love, to let release,
And find in You our perfect peace.

For only You can heal the pain,
And make what's lost be whole again.
Through mercy's gift and love's embrace,
We find our healing in Your grace.

The Shadow of Judas

Beneath the branches of olive trees,
A shadow stirs on the evening breeze.
One of twelve, a chosen friend,
Yet walking now toward bitter end.

A bag of silver, cold and bright,
The price of blood in the dead of night.
Thirty coins, a fleeting gain,
For love betrayed and eternal pain.

He walked with Christ, he knew His face,
He saw the miracles, felt His grace.
But greed and darkness found their way,
To twist his heart, to lead astray.

In the garden's hush, the torches gleam,
A kiss, a signal, ends the dream.
"Rabbi," he whispers, soft and near,
A serpent's touch, betrayal clear.

The soldiers seize, the Teacher bound,
And Judas stands, the silver sounds.
What have I done? His thoughts now cry,
The guilt too vast, the shame too high.

He casts the silver to the floor,
But peace won't come, not anymore.
The noose he ties, his final breath,
Consumed by grief, embraced by death.

Yet even here, a lesson rings,
Of mercy's depths and grace it brings.
For had he sought the Savior's face,
He too could find redeeming grace.

Oh, Judas, shadowed by despair,
Your story warns, your fate lays bare:
That none are lost beyond His call,
If they but turn before they fall.

The Song of Job

A man of honor, upright, true, Whose
faith like morning dew renews. In Uz
he dwelt, with wealth and grace, A
servant of the God of space.

But from the heavens, whispers came, The
Adversary spoke Job's name:
"Does he not serve for gain alone? Take
all he has; his faith will groan."

The tempest rose, the cattle fled, His
children gone, his riches dead.
Yet Job knelt low, in dust and pain, And
praised the Lord through loss and strain.

"The Lord gives life, the Lord takes too,
Blessed be His name, forever true." But
still the trials darkly pressed, Afflicting
body, soul, and rest.

His friends arrived with words of scorn,
"Surely, your guilt is why you mourn.
Repent, confess your hidden sin;
For God is just, His ways within."

 Yet Job held fast, though doubt did creep,
And questioned why his woes ran deep.
Through ash and tear, he sought reply,
And cried aloud to God on high.

Then came the whirlwind, fierce and vast,
Where God spoke truths that ever last:
"Where were you, Job, when earth was
laid? Who calls the stars or storms obeyed?
And all I am belongs to You."

Can you command the ocean's tide?
Or mark where Leviathan might hide? My
wisdom reigns, My power holds,
In every thread the cosmos molds."

Humbled, Job bowed, his voice grown still,
"My Lord, I trust Your sovereign will.
Though pain may blind, Your love is true,
Yet Job held fast, though doubt did creep,
And questioned why his woes ran deep.
Through ash and tear, he sought reply,
And cried aloud to God on high.

Restored was Job, with twice his store,
And blessings filled his life once more.
But greater still, his faith refined, A
beacon for all humankind.

For in his trial, we too may see,
The mystery of God's decree: That
even through the fiercest strife,
He shapes our hearts for eternal life.

The Unexpected Parents

In a humble town, where shadows lay,
A carpenter worked through the light of day.
No throne, no crown, no royal decree,
Just Joseph, a man of quiet dignity.

And Mary, young, with a heart so pure,
Chose faith in a promise unsure.
An angel's word, a heavenly call—
"Bear the Savior, the King of all."

But who were they, this chosen pair,
To cradle God with tender care?
No wealth, no power, no earthly fame,

Yet heaven rejoiced at their simple names.
Through whispered doubts and sideways eyes,
They walked by faith beneath the skies.

To Bethlehem's stable, cold and bare,
Where love was born in the midnight air.
Unexpected, yet divinely known,
Through them, the cornerstone was shown.

For God delights in the lowly and meek,
The hearts of those who humbly seek.
Their story speaks to the grand design—
The ordinary becomes divine.

For in their hands, the world was graced,
With the Son of God, salvation's face.

So ponder well, this holy surprise,
How grace can dwell in the least of lives.
For through their faith, the Savior came,
And through His birth, we're not the same.

The Weight of a Dream

The air feels different now,
A tension in the breeze—
Once, it was light with promise,
Now it carries unease.

We built this dream on fragile ground,
Hoping it would hold,
But now the walls are higher,
And the gates are turning cold.

Voices we once trusted,
Now echo with disdain—
They call us "other," foreign,
As if we're not the same.

What happened to the country,
Where freedom used to ring?
Where dreams were made from nothing,
And hope was everything?

Now, we walk with shoulders hunched,
Not sure which way to turn,
A leader's words like burning coals,
And still, we must return—

To our hopes, to our roots,
To the dreams we've built so far,
Even as the skies grow darker,
And freedom feels ajar.

We carry all the weight of years,
The journey's heavy load,
But we've made this land our home,
And we will walk this road.

No matter who stands at the helm,
Or what the winds may blow,
We are the dreamers, we are the ones—
And we will always go.

Welcoming the Stranger

A stranger stands beyond the door,
A face we've never seen before.
Their eyes hold questions, deep and wide,
Will love invite them safe inside?

The road they walked is rough and long,
A tale of loss, a broken song.
Yet in their steps, the sacred trace
Of one who walks in search of grace.

We hear the call, so soft, so clear:
"Receive the stranger; draw them near.
For when you open heart and hand,
You welcome Me within your land."

A cup of water, bread to share,
A seat prepared with tender care.
These simple acts, so small, so true,
Reflect the love God gives to you.

Remember once, when we were lost,
When fear and exile were the cost.
A stranger's kindness, undeserved,
Revealed a mercy unreserved.

The stranger is a gift unknown,
A chance to make God's love our own.
For in their need, we find our part—
To serve with joy, a willing heart.

So fling the door both wide and free,
And set the table joyfully.
For every stranger we embrace,
Reveals to us the Savior's face.

Through the Shadows, He Sees

In a world of ash and fleeting days,
Where hope seems dim, and hearts dismay,
The path is steep, the valleys deep,
And sorrow wakes where joy should sleep.

Yet through the veil of darkened skies,
A gentle flame, a watchful eye,
Beholds us still, His love ablaze,
To guide our feet through shadowed maze.

He walked the dust, He bore the pain,
Felt every wound, each heavy chain,
And in our tears, He sees His own,
No soul unloved, no heart alone.

When storms arise and tempests roar,
When dreams lie wrecked upon the shore,
His hand extends, His voice is near,
"Be still, my child; I'm always here."

Through thorns that pierce, through trials
long,
He shapes the weak to grow strong.
And though the world may break and fall,
He stands as Savior, Lord of all.

So lift your eyes, though earth may groan,
The cross remains, His love is shown.
In every trial, His grace unfurls—
Jesus sees us through this fallen world.

Voices from the Cross

Thief on the Left

I hang here bound in guilt and shame,

My life a hollow, fleeting flame.

The nails bite deep, the crowd's cruel jeer,

And yet this man—they mock with fear.

He claimed to be the King of light,

But where is mercy in this night?

If you are Christ, then set us free,

Show your power; save yourself and me.

Thief on the Right

I hang condemned, my crimes well known,

A wretched life now overthrown.

Yet here beside me hangs a man,

No guilt, no stain upon His hands.

His eyes hold peace, His face bears grace,

As if He suffers in my place.

Remember me, O Lord, I plea,

When Your kingdom comes, think of me.

Jesus

Forgiven now, for you believed,

This day in paradise you'll be.

One heart will harden, one will break,

The path is yours, the choice to make.

I bear this cross, this pain, this shame,

To free the lost, to call each name.

Through death, through sorrow, love will rise,

To bring salvation, open skies.

Thief on the Left

I mock, I sneer, my heart turns cold,

The truth before me, yet untold.

The sun now fades, the earth does quake,

Too late, my soul begins to ache.

Thief on the Right

The nails still pierce, the thorns still bleed,

But hope now fills my deepest need.

The Savior speaks, and I am whole,

Redeemed at last, my weary soul.

Both Together, Eternities Apart

One chose darkness, one chose light,

Two thieves divided by the night.

The cross remains, the choice is clear,

Eternal love is ever near.